T0157964

Gini Graham Scott, Ph.D.

An Overview of Key Concepts and Methods
in Social Science Research

the
RESEARCHER'S
Bible

iUniverse, Inc.
Bloomington

The Researcher's Bible
An Overview of Key Concepts and Methods in Social Science Research

iUniverse books may be ordered through booksellers or by contacting:

iUniverse
1663 Liberty Drive
Bloomington, IN 47403
www.iuniverse.com
1-800-Authors (1-800-288-4677)

ISBN: 978-1-4620-3777-3 (sc)

Printed in the United States of America

iUniverse rev. date: 08/03/2011

Table of Contents

PART I: AN OVERVIEW OF THE RESEARCH PROCESS   1

WHAT IS RESEARCH AND HOW IT DIFFERS
    FROM PROGRAM EVALUATION AND JOURNALISM 3

WHY IT IS IMPORTANT FOR GRADUATE
    STUDENTS AND PROFESSIONALS TO
    UNDERSTAND OR CONDUCT RESEARCH   6

CHOOSING A RESEARCH TOPIC   8

CONTRIBUTION OF DIFFERENT DISCIPLINES
    TO THE SOCIAL SCIENCES   11

DIFFERENT RESEARCH APPROACHES IN SOCIAL
    SCIENCE RESEARCH   14

**PART II: USING QUALITATIVE AND
QUANTITATIVE RESEARCH METHODS**   19

USING OBSERVATION IN SOCIAL RESEARCH   21

USING QUALITATIVE RESEARCH METHODS   25

USING QUANTITATIVE RESEARCH METHODS   27

PART III: USING SAMPLING METHODS   31

THE MAIN CHARACTERISTICS OF SAMPLING
    METHODS   33

THE ADVANTAGES AND DISADVANTAGES OF
    DIFFERENT SAMPLING METHODS   35

AN IDEAL SAMPLING TECHNIQUE FOR SOCIAL
    RESEARCH   39

PART IV: ANALYZING STUDY RESULTS   41

THE MAIN TECHNIQUES FOR ANALYZING
SURVEYS AND THEIR ADVANTAGES AND
DISADVANTAGES   43

THE MAJOR STATISTICAL CONCEPTS   47

THE MAJOR DATA ANALYSIS TECHNIQUES   51

THE EASIEST METHOD FOR SOCIAL RESEARCH   56

About the Author

Gini Graham Scott has published over 50 books, focusing on social trends using a number of research methods, from in-depth interviews and participant observation to surveys and secondary research. Some of these books include:

- *The Very Next New Thing* (ABC-Clio 2011)
- *Playing the Lying Game* (ABC-Clio 2010)
- *The Talk Show Revolution* (ASJA Press 2008, previously published as *Can We Talk?: The Power and Influence of Talk Shows*, Plenum 1996),
- *The Privacy Revolution* (ASJA Press 2008, previously published as *Mind Your Own Business: The Battle for Personal Privacy*, Plenum 1995),
- *Fantasy Worlds* (ASJA Press 2007, previously published *The Power of Fantasy*, Wiley).

She received a Ph.D. in Sociology from the University of California and MAs in Anthropology, Mass Communications and Organizational/ Consumer and Audience Behavior, and Pop Culture and Lifestyles from California State University, East Bay. She is currently working towards an MS in Recreation and Tourism, expected in 2012.

She has an extensive background in market research, including three years working for Foote, Cone, and Belding as a project manager. She conducted a study on Investigating Homicide Patterns in Oakland that was published by the Oakland Police Department, and conducted two surveys on the arts community in Oakland for Pro Arts, an organization of about 1000 artists.

She has gained extensive media interest for previous books, including appearances on *Good Morning America*, *Oprah*, *Montel Williams*, *CNN*, and hundreds of radio interviews. She has frequently been quoted by the media and has set up websites to promote her most recent books, including: www.workingwithhumans.com, www.workwithgini.com, and www.badbosses.net.

Additional bio and promotional material is at her website at www. ginigrahamscott.com and at www.behaviorresearch.net.

Introduction

THE RESEARCHER'S BIBLE provides an overview of the major social research methods and when to use different approaches. It offers a quick summary of the different possible approaches and their major advantages and disadvantages, so a researcher can better decide which techniques to use for a particular project. As such, it makes an ideal supplement to more comprehensive research books used by professors, students, and researchers in the social sciences to summarize the main concepts and methodologies in the field. The book might also be a useful guide for professionals to give to clients to explain the different research procedures, so the clients understand why a researcher wants to use a selected technique.

The topics covered include:

- the contributions of different disciples,

- different research approaches,

- using observation,

- qualitative and quantitative research methods,

- the main sampling methods and their advantages and disadvantages,

- the best sampling techniques for different types of research projects,

- major statistical concepts and data analysis techniques,

- the most useful statistical methods for different types of research

The book is divided into four sections:

1. an overview of the research process,

2. using qualitative and quantitative research methods

3. using sampling methods

4. analyzing study results.

PART I

An Overview of the Research Process

CHAPTER 1

WHAT IS RESEARCH AND HOW IT DIFFERS FROM PROGRAM EVALUATION AND JOURNALISM

Research is based on discovering something that is previously unknown, and it is a tool or technique used by science to increase human knowledge. If it is scientific research, it is designed to follow the rules of science which are based on logic and reason. To this end, it systematically looks at evidence and assesses how valuable it is to add to the knowledge about a particular subject matter. Another characteristic of research is that it should be possible for others to replicate the research and achieve similar results if it is practical to conduct another study.

To some extent, any social research can be based on this scientific model. However, since social research is the study of people and their behavior, the scientific model has to be adapted to take into consideration that people are less predictable. Also, when study subjects realize they are being researched, they may adapt their behavior, such as to conceal any negative attitudes and behaviors and present themselves in a positive light. Then, too, the research of subjects is affected by the culture and social norms, values, beliefs, and expectations of their own culture. Thus, for all these reasons, social research studies may not be replicable, as is the case for scientific studies.

However, social research differs from regular reporting and journalism in that it is designed to follow scientific rules and contribute to and build on knowledge in a particular area. Research also differs from journalism in that it describes patterns and explains them based on looking at multiple cases of some phenomenon. Another distinction is that social research involves drawing inductive conclusions from a series of facts or starting with a hypothesis and deducing conclusions based on whether a hypothesis can be proved or not.

Another difference from social research is that journalism looks at particular cases of something to report a news story. Also, journalism tends to look for what's new or novel, and it features differences or unusual examples of something to attract reader or viewer interest. Journalism is also often transitory, as journalists leap on one story after another, as the news changes from day to day, whereas researchers seek to contribute to a particular body of knowledge. In some cases, journalists may report the results of research as a story of interest to viewers or readers, but journalists generally do not conduct the research themselves to find the patterns and explanations; they generally report what researchers in a field of study have done.

Much social research differs from program evaluation in that most social research is descriptive or explanatory. As such, this research is used to find out or describe what is, based on looking for behavior patterns and trends, such as the participation over time in an activity by different groups of people. By contrast, explanatory research is used to explain why certain patterns have occurred; and it uses these findings to predict what might be.

While program evaluation is a form of research, it uses research methods to study how well a particular policy or program is doing, it is focused on assessing the success or effectiveness of a current program and making recommendations based on study results, such as whether to continue a program or end it. Another difference between program evaluation and other social research is that much social research is conducted by independent researchers according to accepted methodologies, whereas a program evaluation is not always done by an independent researcher. Rather it is often undertaken by the agency or organization seeking the evaluator is conducted in response to political factors, so that the results might be influenced by the agency or organization heads or by government officials. This influence can occur because the results of the evaluation can determine whether a program continues to get funding or whether an agency or organization head will continue to lead the agency or organization – a situation I experienced when I worked as an evaluation researcher for several criminal justice organizations for two years. Since I was being paid by the organizations being evaluated – a clear conflict of interest, I had to adapt my results to satisfy the heads of the agencies.

CHAPTER 2

WHY IT IS IMPORTANT FOR GRADUATE STUDENTS AND PROFESSIONALS TO UNDERSTAND OR CONDUCT RESEARCH

It is important for graduate students and professionals to understand or conduct research for several reasons.

Graduate students need this ability, since they will often have to cite research in writing papers or doing projects. They need to be able to understand the results, so they can build on this information in doing their own research. They should also be able to evaluate how the research was done to assess the value of the research results.

For example, if a study is badly conducted, this can call into question the validity of the results. Graduate students also need to understand research to design their own studies and shape their research designs. This ability is especially important for students interested in academic careers, because they will normally be expected to conduct research studies and publish the results in peer reviewed journals. Their peers will be critical of how well they have done the research supporting their results.

Professionals need to understand research to help them with their day to day work in their social science field, such as if they want to conduct or commission research to look at who is participating in their programs or how to expand their programs to other geographic areas. If they design the research effectively, they will gain accurate results they can use to make effective decisions on running or expanding their programs. They may also want to look at the research results of others in their field to look at the patterns and trends discovered to help in making decisions about their own programs. Understanding how the research was conducted by others can help them assess the accuracy of the results, and they can use this assessment to guide their own decisions.

Understanding research can also help professionals hire an outside researcher or research team to conduct the research for them, since they will know what questions to ask to determine the researchers' competency. Understanding research can also help professionals work with a researcher or research team by shaping their research questions, so they learn the needed information to make good decisions. This understanding can also help in preparing good articles for professional journals that contribute to one's credibility and thereby one's career.

CHAPTER 3

CHOOSING A RESEARCH TOPIC

The main reasons for choosing a research topic are:

- personal interest, in which a researcher is personally involved in a particular activity, such as a sport or hobby, already has knowledge of the field, or has access to key individuals or information sources. This personal interest can provide a high level of motivation to know more about the subject.

- a review of the literature, which is the most common basis for choosing a topic by academic researchers. This review can be an ideal basis for rationally choosing a topic, since it can suggest ways to further test and explore a theory, examine how a theory applies in a different country or region, apply a theory from one social science to another, or investigate the applicability of the theory using a different method.

- a policy or management rationale, supplied by an organization or agency or by a researcher interested in policy or management issues. Such research might not only be applied to a particular program, but more generally to other programs.

- a social concern, to examine issues dealing with the members of social groups that have been deprived or neglected. Such research might be used to draw attention to a group's needs or problems, and it might help resolve these difficulties, once they are recognized.

- <u>a response to a popular issue or topic featured in the media</u> to explore it further or to correct inaccuracies in a popular presentation.

- <u>a response to research agendas</u>, which are published by professional organizations or individual academics, describing topics on which they would like research information.

- <u>brainstorming</u>, whereby two or more people come up with ideas that inspire them.

Regardless of how a researcher decides on a topic, the researcher still needs to provide a rationale basis for choosing the topic by relating it to a review of the literature and to the theory in the field. The process is much like what happens when a judge makes a decision based on emotional or intuitive gut feelings. He or she has to justify that decision by finding a rationale basis to support it.

Commonly, the researcher will explain this reasoning in the introduction to their paper.

For example, as described in "The Impact of Participation in an Inclusive Adventure Education Trip on Group Dynamics," Sue Sutherland and Sandra Stroot explained that they conducted an ethnographic case study to examine the impact of participating in an inclusive 3-day rock climbing trip on the group dynamics of seven participants, age 10 to 14. They also explained that they would apply Tuchman's five-stage group development model, first proposed in 1965, which suggests that a group goes through the stages of forming, storming, norming, conforming, and adjourning. Sutherland and Stroot wanted to see if that model would apply in an adventure education (AE) program designed to help the students feel an increased level of self-awareness, self-esteem, self-confidence, trust, cooperation with others, and better communication and problem solving skills. They chose Tuchman's five stage model to guide them in designing and analyzing the study, since the model hadn't been used before to examine participation and group dynamics in such an inclusive AE experience, thereby expanding the model to another area of research.

In another case, described in "You don't want to hurt his feelings...' Family Leisure as a Context for Intergenerational Ambivalence," Shannon Hebblewaite and Joan E. Norris decided to look at the role of intergenerational ambivalence in the family leisure experience of grandparents and their adult grandchildren by interviewing the members of fourteen sets of grandparents and their adult grandchildren. They chose this topic since leisure activities play an important role in family bonding, and they found that most family leisure research looked at the benefits of participating in these activities, such as improved communication among family members and improved cohesiveness and strength. But this family leisure research largely ignored conflict and the role of older adults, so they felt a need to better understand the potential for negative experiences and the grandparent-grandchild relationship given increasing longevity today.

Thus, as these examples illustrate, the researchers introduced their own research by discussing their reasons for conducting their study by drawing on the research of others to show gaps in the research they wanted to fill. Then, they described the concepts and methods they wanted to apply in their own studies in another topics area.

CHAPTER 4

CONTRIBUTION OF DIFFERENT DISCIPLINES TO THE SOCIAL SCIENCES

The social sciences, including leisure and tourism studies, are characterized by a diversity of approaches from different disciplines and a variety of methods. As a result, social science studies in some fields, like leisure and tourism, use an inter-disciplinary or multi-disciplinary approach by drawing on different frames of reference and different methodological approaches for conducting studies.

To this end, researchers should consider the research questions they want to answer based on the purpose of their research. For instance, do they want to do a study to build on the academic store of knowledge or conduct a study for a professional client or business organization for marketing purposes? A researcher might regard these different approaches like a tool-kit to draw on, as appropriate, for conducting a study for a particular purpose.

The approaches of the different disciplines include these.

- the sociological approach, which has provided much of the foundation for social science research, including recreation and leisure . The sociological approach involves three major thrusts. One is doing social surveys, some which are for pragmatic reasons and are considered social research rather than academically-oriented sociological research. These surveys involve a quantitative approach, based on using statistics and mathematical models of human behavior to make predictions about human behavior. This is sometimes called the "surveys and modeling approach."

A second sociological approach seeks to explain why people behave as they do in choosing their activities; it looks at the meaning of their participation or non-participation in different types of activities for different groups of people. One approach to discovering meaning is the existential and symbolic interaction approach, which considers the way people negotiate their participation in light of different types of relationships – from personal and social relationships to their relationship with their community and their networks at work.

A third sociological approach is the critical approach which has taken various forms. One is the neo-Marxist approach, which looks at the way in which individuals can act freely or are constrained and influenced by the structure of their society. A key aspect of neo-Marxism has been criticizing the capitalist system for exploiting or manipulating people within the system who have little power. Numerous streams of critical theory have influenced this perspective over the last few decades, including the feminist perspective, which has considered the way women have responded to leisure and other types of activities in light of their lesser power in society. Another critical approach is postmodernism, which has explored the role of electronic communications and the cultural artifacts it has produced. Postmodern researchers have been especially interested in the content of these expressions of culture rather than in the behavior of the people creating cultural artifacts.

- the geographic approach, which has examined the way spaces and landscapes affect people's behavior and their perception of those spaces and landscapes, especially in making choices about their travel behavior. Geographers also look how people use different kinds of spaces and leisure facilities, such as national parks, gardens, playgrounds, and sports facilities.

- the economic approach, which looks at the economic valuation of different kinds of activities and facilities, such as outdoor recreation areas and arts facilities. One way researchers using this approach have measured results is by doing a cost-benefits analysis to examine the costs and benefits of particular facilities and programs to the public. Researchers have also examined the way pricing different activities and programs has affected demand, and the researchers have done demand forecasting studies to examine how much consumers are likely to spend on different activities and programs in a particular location.

- the psychology/social psychology approach, which looks at people's satisfactions and negative experiences from various activities, their motivations leading them to participate in an activity, how their relationships with others influences their participation, and how their perceptions affect their involvement in these activities. In particular, these researchers do research in four main areas: motivation and needs, satisfactions, the individual's state of mind, and the way personal characteristics, such as gender, age, culture, and personality affect participation. These researchers commonly use self-completion questionnaires to survey their subjects, such as consumers, visitors to an event, and college students.

- the historical approach, which looks at historical trends, particularly in the U.S., Canada, and Europe.

- the anthropological approach, which has been especially interested in the effect of modern influences and tourism on indigenous cultures and low-income and underserved populations.

- the political science approach, which not only analyzes the political system but examines the politics of interpersonal dynamics in an organization. It also considers the politics of making decisions about participating in leisure and other activities in a particular locale and has explored the way tourism and other activities affect political behavior.

CHAPTER 5

DIFFERENT RESEARCH APPROACHES
IN SOCIAL SCIENCE RESEARCH

Besides the approach of different disciplines, a dozen approaches involve more than one discipline. These are:

- the theoretical approach, which draws a general conclusion about the subject being studied, and thereby contributes to the growing body of research in different fields.

- the applied research approach, which applies the theoretical knowledge that already exists to specific areas of concern, such as in the area of policy, planning, or management, which each have developed their own theories.

- the empirical research approach, which involves collecting and analyzing different types of quantitative and qualitative data and examining both primary data collected by the researcher and secondary data obtained from other sources. Such research is designed to obtain data from the everyday world, though commonly the data has a theoretical or non-empirical aspect, too.

- the inductive approach, which involves gathering data from observation, describing and analyzing that information, and explaining the results of that analysis.

- the deductive approach, whereby the researcher starts with a hypothesis about how something might be expected to act. To test that hypothesis, the researcher makes observations and analyzes these findings to determine if they support the hypothesis or not, usually by creating a null hypothesis and trying to disprove that. To this end, the researcher uses probabilities at a certain level, commonly the 95% level, to indicate whether the null hypothesis can be rejected, since it is probably incorrect, and therefore the research hypothesis is probably correct at that probability level.

- the descriptive approach, which describes what is, as best the researchers can describe it, such as a pattern of behavior.

- the explanatory approach, which suggests why something has occurred, commonly by showing that one thing caused another to happen. To show this is a real association, not just due to coincidences, the following are required to show a sufficiently high level of connection at the required level of probability: a time priority whereby one thing takes place before another; a nonspurious relationship, whereby the relationship between two variables can't be explained by a third variable; and a good rationale, which provides a reasonable explanation of why the two variables are related. For example, two things might repeatedly occur together, but there is no logical reason they are connected or cause each other, such as an increase of obesity in the United States at the same time that travel to South America is on the increase.

- the positivist or outside research approach, in which researchers gather facts and observations about the way people behave and draw on theories and models to explain this behavior.

- the interpretive or inside research approach, whereby researchers look at the way the people being studied view their own behavior or situation.

- the experimental approach, in which the researcher creates an experimental condition that affects the environment or a situation the research subject is experiencing. The researcher then seeks to examine the effects of that condition on the subject, commonly by comparing the subjects in the experimental condition to subjects in a control group who haven't been affected by that condition. For example, a researcher can select certain stimuli for a control group, such as seeing a photo or video or participating in a certain activity. Then, the researcher can compare the reactions of the groups in the control condition with the responses of others not subjected to the stimuli.

- the non-experimental approach, in which the researcher looks at any differences which already exist between individuals or groups, rather than trying to manipulate different groups using an experimental method.

- the primary data approach, which is based on the researcher collecting new information.

- the secondary data approach, which is based on using existing data, such as when a researcher takes statistics collected by someone else and analyzes them to look for patterns or trends.

- the self-reported data approach, in which people make reports about themselves, such as when a researcher asks people what they have done in the past or about their attitudes and goals for the future.

- the observed data approach, in which the researcher makes observations of what people are actually doing, in contrast to having them self-report what they are doing.

- the qualitative research approach, in which a researcher collects information about a small number of people, using observation, informal and in-depth interviewing, and participant observation. This approach is called ethnographic fieldwork when used to study a group. While this approach was developed by anthropologists, it is commonly used by sociologists.

- the quantitative research approach, based on doing a statistical analysis of data collected from a large number of people, such as from a survey with questions asking for numerical ratings or rankings.

There is an overlap between the disciplines and the types of approaches used, though differences in the extent to which these methods are used in difference social sciences. For example, sociologists tend to use more of the statistical quantitative approaches and anthropologists more of the qualitative observational approaches, but both may use either approach at different times. A social researcher can draw on different disciplines and approaches to decide on the best approach or combination of approaches for a particular study.

PART II

Using Qualitative And Quantitative Research Methods

CHAPTER 6

USING OBSERVATION IN SOCIAL RESEARCH

Observation involves looking at a particular setting in various ways. These range from informally watching what is going on to structuring the observation, such as by noting what is observed at particular times or counting the number of people, vehicles, or behavior at a site. In some cases, an observer can watch unobtrusively, like an ordinary bystander, without identifying him or herself to the people being observed. In other cases, the observer can participate while observing the behavior, either with the other participants' knowledge or without their knowledge when they think the observer is just another group member. Such observation can occur with the observer noting only what is seen with the naked eye; in other cases, the observer can use special equipment, such as time-lapse photography, aerial photography, or a video camera to take pictures of the behavior.

The major situations where observation is more appropriate than other methods include:

- observing child's play, such as to determine the type of play activities or equipment children prefer or to identify differences in the play of different children, such as boys and girls or children from different ethnic groups. Child's play is best observed, since it can be difficult to interview and get answers from children, especially the very young, since they don't have the verbal ability or may not feel comfortable talking to an adult interviewer;

- <u>assessing the usage patterns in informal settings</u>, such as at a recreational site where there is no entrance charge, so the staff has no way to control access or obtain a count, such as by collecting tickets or installing a pay gate to enter the area. Assessing usage patterns by observation might also be useful if most visitors arrive by car, even with a per vehicle charge, since the number of people can vary for each vehicle;

- <u>determining the way people use the site</u>, based on where they go or what activities they engage in;

- <u>determining the demographic characteristics or developing a user profile</u>, since a brief questionnaire might not provide this information or show how different types of people use the facility differently;

- <u>describing deviant behavior</u>, since people may not want to talk to an interviewer or answer a questionnaire about any behavior considered deviant, since it is unacceptable or against the rules;

- <u>observing consumer behavior or the experience consumers have</u> in a store or leisure facility, such as by being a mystery shopper or guest. Such observation might be useful to assess the quality of the services consumers receive or notice how consumers respond to in-store displays and make purchases;

- <u>conducting observations as complementary research</u> to support quantitative findings or counteract the effects of variations in sampling patterns due to changing circumstances. For example, there could be sampling variation when more individuals are interviewed or respond to a questionnaire at one time of day and fewer do so at another time, since there could be differences in the attitudes, lifestyles, and demographics between the two groups. For instance, more families with kids may go to a recreational site during the day and more single adults may go there in the early evening;

- observing the way people behave and interact in everyday life, such as when sociologist Erving Goffman distinguished between the way people engaged in different types of behavior in public and in private spaces;

- making observations to develop theories about how people behave in different social environments, such as by using induction to make inferences from one's observations and then using those inferences to build theories.

The choice of what methods to use depends on the topic and expected outcome of a study. For example, say you wanted to study the variation in the attitudes, motivation, perception of value in a new start-up entertainment business by race, ethnicity, culture, and gender, you might do the following.

- You could either observe the users' demographic characteristics or profiles by being present when consumers use the service, or you could train employees to note these characteristics for each customer. Using observation to obtain demographic information about the consumers' age, gender, race, and ethnicity at different times and days could be helpful in identifying different target markets to better market and promote the service to these groups. However, it would be best to make these observations with the naked eye rather than using a camera or video recorder, since consumers might feel uncomfortable being photographed while using the service, and it would be an unethical violation of the expected privacy to have hidden cameras.

- You could observe the way consumers behave in a store or other area and notice the interaction between the consumer and service provider. Such observation might be useful for quality control to assess how well the consumer enjoys the experience and whether the employees are effective in providing the service. Also, this observation might be related to how the customer rates the service on a questionnaire and whether the customer uses the service again.

- You could observe how people behave and interact when they use the service or participate in any activity. You also might observe how people learn about a service or participate in an activity, such as a trade show or business fair, which might help in improving the methods of attracting people to use a service, as well as improve it.

- Finally, you could make observations to develop theories about how different types of people behave in and experience different social environments. For example, businessmen experiencing a service at a conference or trade show might differ from women experiencing it at a shopping mall, while teenagers experiencing the service at a party or community center might differ from older adults experiencing it at a restaurant or bar. Observing the different behaviors might help to develop theories about different motivations and value perceptions of different types of consumers in different settings.

CHAPTER 7

USING QUALITATIVE RESEARCH METHODS

Qualitative research methods are characterized by collecting a lot of in-depth or "rich" information about a small number of cases. Such research involves looking at the key issues from the viewpoint of the people involved in the study. To obtain information using the qualitative approach, the researcher asks people to describe their experiences or feelings in their own words and explain why they behaved in a certain way.

The methods used in this approach include in-depth interviews, focus groups, participant observation, analyzing texts, biographical research, and ethnography.

The qualitative research approach has a number of merits for certain types of studies, such as conducting a small scale study with a limited number of subjects or studying the group dynamics in a small group. One advantage of qualitative research in such situations is that the research reflects the meanings which the activity has to the individual. Another advantage is that this research provides a more personal approach than quantitative research to the subject studied. A third benefit is that the results can be better understood by the average person who doesn't understand statistical methods -- a common characteristic of many people heading up companies, non-profits, government agencies, and recreational programs. Often they don't do their own studies and hire researchers to conduct their studies and advise them.

The qualitative approach is ideal for looking at trends over time and at the influences of past experiences on present behavior. This approach is also well suited to examining the cultural aspects of interaction, such as the meanings of the symbols and gestures of people from different backgrounds. This distinction is important because people from different cultures may interpret language, symbols, and gestures differently. For instance, while one culture considers a certain hand gesture as a sign of friendship, another culture considers the same gesture as a put down or insult.

Qualitative research additionally can help in developing a hypothesis about the relationship between certain attitudes, values, and behaviors; and one can later use quantitative research to test these hypotheses. Qualitative research is ideal for doing a pilot or exploratory study to determine the major issues, attitudes, values, perceptions, and viewpoints to examine further in a quantitative study. Qualitative research might also be used to indicate the relevant categories or subjects to include in a larger study, as well as the questions to ask. It can additionally help a researcher determine the right words and phrases to use in asking questions of members of a particular group or culture in order to use words in common usage by group members and to show that one understands that culture.

The main disadvantages of the qualitative approach are these. It can't be used to test hypotheses, because it involves a very small number of subjects. It can't be subjected to the kind of reliability and validity testing done in quantitative research, such as when subjects are randomly selected for the study or when an experimental design with control and experimental groups is used. Another disadvantage is that the results can't be generalized to a larger group, since the study subjects are not selected to be representative of a larger group, which is expected when a randomized sample is used in a large quantitative study. Another problem is that when a researcher studies a small group, such as through participant observation, the researcher's presence might influence the behavior and attitudes of group members. For instance, in a study of deviant behavior, the group members may avoid participating in certain activities, because they don't want to reveal them to a researcher considered an outsider, even if he or she participates in group activities like other group members.

CHAPTER 8

USING QUANTITATIVE RESEARCH METHODS

Quantitative research methods are characterized by collecting limited information about a large number of cases. The most common method for doing this in social research is using a questionnaire survey or interview schedule based on asking a series of already created questions. These questions can either be asked by an interviewer in an interviewer completion survey or by the subject in a respondent completion survey. The questions can be pre-coded, so that the interviewee or respondent chooses among a range of responses, or they can be open-ended, so the subject can answer in his or her own words, and the answer can be coded or analyzed later.

Commonly, a survey involves asking questions of a percentage or sample of the larger population, using various sampling techniques to get a representative sample, such as a random sample or quota sample. Once the surveys are completed, the data from each question is combined to provide numerical data for that question. The data can then be analyzed through various quantitative methods, such as comparing the percentages of responses of different groups of respondents to different questions, obtaining an average or median for rating or ranking data, or doing a correlation or regression analysis.

The methods used in quantitative research include:

- a household survey, in which people are interviewed in their home and are selected to be included in the survey based on their location;

- a street survey, in which people are stopped on the street or in a shopping mall and asked the survey questions;

- a telephone survey, in which the interviewer calls the prospective survey participant.

- a mail survey, in which the interviewee receives a questionnaire in the mail and is asked to return it;

- an e-survey, in which a person is invited to participate in a survey on a website or sent the questions by e-mail;

- a user survey (sometimes called a site or visitor survey) in which a user of a recreation or other facility or a tourist is asked questions about the location just visited;

- a captive group survey, in which the members of a group, employees of an organization, or students in a school are asked to participate in a survey and normally are required to do so because they are members of that group.

A questionnaire survey has many advantages for certain types of studies, such as for collecting information from a large number of people. This approach is often appropriate for studies for large organizations making policy and management decisions about how to deal with large populations using its services. Another virtue of a questionnaire survey is that it shows how the information was collected and analyzed, so the results can be reanalyzed or the same procedures used to replicate the study with other subjects. Then, the results of different surveys over time can be compared to notice any differences or look for trends.

The questionnaire survey approach is also good for taking a large amount of data and presenting it in a simple, compact form, so others can readily understand it, including government officials making policy decisions and managers deciding on management policies and procedures. The ease of analysis occurs because hundreds or thousands of ratings or rankings can be combined into a single average or median for different groups of respondents. Then, the responses of these different groups can be easily compared, such as to indicate that people from different age groups rate certain activities differently.

A series of surveys can be used to obtain longitudinal data to examine trends over time, and the results can be conveyed through graphs or charts. Surveys can also provide a comprehensive picture of the activities engaged in by different types of people, as well as provide an overall view of the types of attitudes, perceptions, and meanings held by different groups by using Likert scales, semantic differentials, checklists, rankings, and attitude statements. The activities, attitudes, perceptions, and meanings of different groups of people can then be compared based on these overall measures.

However, surveys do have a number of disadvantages. One disadvantage is that it can be difficult to get a representative sample, since the people answering the survey may differ from those who don't respond. Another problem is that the questions on a pre-coded survey may not reflect the full range of responses, while many people may not answer or fully answer an open-ended question. A further problem is that people may not answer the survey questions honestly, because they want to conceal negative information, or they may provide overly positive answers, since they want to please the interviewer.

Still another problem with surveys is that increasingly, people may be unwilling to respond to surveys, because they resent the intrusion on the phone or at their home, or they don't want to take the time to respond. They may also hesitate to answer because they distrust the interviewer, especially if they think the interviewer on the phone is a salesperson trying to sell them something or think the interviewer at their door is a criminal casing the neighborhood or trying to rob them. Some people never respond to phone or door-to-door surveys, and some even have a "no soliciting" sign on their door, making it illegal to ring their bell. Many people don't respond to interviewers in shopping centers, because they are in a hurry. Thus, researchers are likely to find that those willing to respond to surveys are different from those who don't.

Another disadvantage of surveys is that they have to be short to get any response -- generally 5 minutes for an intercept survey or

10-15 minutes for a phone interview, so it may be necessary to leave out important questions. Questionnaires also can't get at the deeper meanings and attitudes that people have. Rather, a more qualitative probing approach is necessary to obtain such information. Moreover, since surveys depend on the respondents' recall, errors can occur in what they remember, particularly when they have to remember back further in time, such as when asked what activities they participated in and how often in the past few days, week, month or a year or more ago. Additionally, respondents may be reluctant to give out sensitive information, such as on their income, on a questionnaire or to an interviewer they don't know.

PART III

USING SAMPLING METHODS

CHAPTER 9

THE MAIN CHARACTERISTICS
OF SAMPLING METHODS

A sample is a small group drawn from a larger population, and it should be as representative as possible of this population. To this end a number of random sampling methods are used to avoid a biased sample. The main sampling methods used to create a representative sample are these.

- <u>Sampling using a household survey</u>. This sampling approach involves taking a survey of households drawn from the total population of a country or region, since it is unrealistic to list everyone in the country or region. Everyone has a equal chance of being drawn through the sampling process, and commonly a multi-stage and clustered sampling approach is used. In the multi-staged approach, the sample is divided into sections, such as regions, and subsamples are selected from voter records or streets in the area. Every nth house on the street is selected, such as every third, fourth, or fifth house, to obtain the desired number of houses to be included. Then, the person in that household matching the criteria for inclusion, such as being the head of household or the oldest female, is included in the survey.

- <u>Sampling for a site, user, or visitor survey</u>. This sampling approach involves drawing a sample from the users of a product or service or from participants in an activity or event. This sampling can be done by a stationery interviewer who interviews a sampling of users or visitors as they pass by, such as when an interviewer stands at the entrance or exit of a shopping mall or amusement park. Alternatively, the interviewer can be mobile and interview a sampling of stationery users, such as visitors at a park campsite or barbecue area. In either case, the interviewer can introduce randomness by following certain rules, such as when a stationery interviewer interviews every nth person passing a location or when a mobile interviewer interviews every nth person he or she passes while walking along a particular route.

- Quota sampling, usually in a street survey. This sampling approach is based on seeking a preselected number or quota of people of a certain type, so they will represent a designated percentage of the targeted population. Researchers use this quota approach to obtain a broad sampling of different type of people in a population, when the population breakdown is known. This method might be used when a researcher can't get a representative sampling by other means, such as when the targeted members of the population are less receptive to surveys or more difficult to find. An example might be sampling lower class individuals who are less likely to be home when an interviewer comes to do an interview. A quota sample is called a street survey, when the interviewees are contacted on the street or while shopping in a mall.

- Sampling for a mail survey. This sampling approach is based on sending a survey to people by mail or e-mail. Recipients are asked to fill in the survey through self-completion and return it, usually in a pre-addressed and often pre-stamped envelope, by return e-mail, or by following an online link to fill in the survey.

CHAPTER 10

THE ADVANTAGES AND DISADVANTAGES OF DIFFERENT SAMPLING METHODS

The advantages and disadvantages of using different sampling methods include these.

Household Survey Method

The advantage of the household survey method is that it provides a sample of an entire population of a country or region. Such a survey might be good if one wants to know what people throughout the area are thinking, such as by obtaining opinions on an issue to help a politician take a position on a bill for a new enterprise zone, park, or transportation improvements. Such as survey might also be good for the government to learn about people's preferences about a new community center or recreational facility, such as whether they would prefer a zoo or nature park and who would be interested in going.

A disadvantage of the household survey is that it is very time-consuming and laborious to obtain a sampling of everyone in the whole population. Also, while most organizations doing national surveys use multi-stage and clustered sampling to make gathering the sample more manageable, there can be problems in doing so. For example, if researchers try to reduce costs by interviewing a certain number of people on the street or choosing every nth house, they could make the number of clusters too small to include a complete variety of people who live in the area. Additionally, the researchers might find that people in certain types of households might not want to participate in the survey, most notably those from lower-class homes, who often fear outsiders as government officials, social workers, or the police. Their lack of participation would skew the sample to having a greater percentage of middle and high income people than their percentage in the population.

Site, User, or Visitor survey

The advantage of sampling for a site, user, or visitor survey is that one can obtain feedback from a population using that facility or site. Another advantage is that one can control for randomness by having a trained interviewer select either the nth person passing the interviewer or the nth person the interviewer passes after interviewing a previous selected person. This site approach can also be adapted to be used as a quota sample, whereby the interviewer seeks out the nth person for a number of categories and stops looking for someone for a category after filling that a category.

A disadvantage of this site approach is that an interviewer may fail to follow procedures about selecting interviews and might select someone who seems convenient or not include interviewees who are more difficult to find or interview. Another disadvantage is that the type of individuals coming at different times of day may vary, such as having more families with kids coming during the day and teenagers coming at night to an amusement park. As a result, the sampling could become unrepresentative, unless it is weighted or a quota sampling approach is used to balance out the different types of people coming at different times.

Another disadvantage of this approach might be a high level of non-responses, if people entering or leaving the site don't want to be bothered – those entering because they are eager to enjoy the site and those leaving because they are eager to get home. Still another disadvantage of a site survey if a questionnaire is used is that many respondents may not complete the questionnaire, and those who do may be unrepresentative of the whole group, particularly when there is a high return rate. Then, too, personnel at the site may not carefully hand out the questionnaires, and it may be difficult to supervise the employees, since their priority is to help visitors and guests, rather than help with a survey.

Street Survey and Quota Sampling

The advantage of using sampling for a street survey is that one can find out who is using a particular street, shopping, or tourist area, much like determining who is going to a particular site with a site, user, or visitor survey. A street survey can also be combined with quota sampling to obtain information on different types of users or visitors to the area at different times.

However, the disadvantage of a street survey, much like a site, user, or visitor survey, is that people on the street might be busy and not want to take time to participate in an interview or fill out a questionnaire. As a result, the sample will be biased due to differences between those who answer questions and those who don't.

Another disadvantage is the possible danger of stopping and interviewing people on the street in some areas. For instance, in an inner city area, people may be suspicious of outsiders, thinking they might be government workers or undercover cops, so they don't want to answer questions. The interviewers or those distributing questionnaires might also be in danger of being threatened or attacked.

As for quota sampling, a disadvantage is that this method can't be used if one doesn't already know the background of the people in the area to draw up quotas. Then, too, if people don't want to take the time to respond to a street survey, very few will respond to and return a take-home survey, so the survey will have a low response rate and it will be hard to fill the quotas.

A disadvantage of doing a quota survey by e-mail is that not only may the response rate be low, but certain types of people are less likely to use email, such as lower-income individuals. To compensate for this problem, weighting is often used with quota surveys to get a sample that corresponds more closely to the percentage of that group in the larger population.

Mail and E-Mail Surveys

The advantage of doing sampling using the regular mails is that this can be used for a large completely random survey, since the mail generally goes to everyone in the population. However, a disadvantage is that it can be expensive to mail a survey to a large group. Another disadvantage is the normally high non-response rate to mailed questionnaires, and those who respond may be different from those who don't.

While the cost factor can be reduced substantially with an email survey, the disadvantage is that those with e-mails or most likely to respond to e-mails may differ from the population that doesn't respond and from those who don't have emails -- usually those with a lower income.

CHAPTER 11

AN IDEAL SAMPLING TECHNIQUE
FOR SOCIAL RESEARCH

An ideal sampling technique for much social research, especially for leisure, tourism, entertainment, and shopping venues, is the site/user/ or visitor survey using interviews to get information about usage or attitudes for a location or facility. This approach is well suited for getting this information, since one can obtain the response of those already using the site.

This approach can be adapted to overcome some of the problems that might occur in using this method. For instance, one can carefully train interviewers on the procedures to identify the appropriate people to interview, and one can carefully supervise and monitor the interviewers to make sure they are selecting people and conducting the interviews correctly. If not, one can provide the interviewers with more training or terminate any interviewers who still don't follow the protocol.

One can also train the interviewers to know what to say to prospective interviewees to increase the response rate. One might also increase the response rate by offering the visitors and attendees an incentive for taking a few minutes to respond to the survey, such as offering a free pass in a prize drawing to the site or to a future event.

It is also possible to avoid the problem of interviewers not being able to interview every nth person at an entrance, when people arrive at different times or in large crowd by changing the procedure, so the interviewer interviews every nth person after completing an interview. Another possibility is having additional interviewers when an area is more crowded, so they can interview the next person selected if another interviewer is busy. In this way, a pool of interviewers can be available to respond as users, visitors, attendees or tourists arrive.

Using an interview with this sampling approach is a good strategy, since one can avoid the high non-response rate for respondent completion questionnaires. The cost of the interviewers can be kept down by using student interns or volunteers from community civic groups, who may often work at no charge or at a low rate because they find interviewing at an event or recreational or tourist facility to be a fun activity, and may do it in return for academic credit or the experience.

This sampling to learn about site usage and the attitudes of users, visitors, or attendees is much more targeted and cost effective than other sampling methods, such as household surveys or mailed surveys. These can be very expensive and can include many non-users. However, a household or mail survey would be more appropriate to find out why non-users aren't going to that site or event or their attitudes towards different types of recreation.

PART IV

ANALYZING STUDY RESULTS

CHAPTER 12

THE MAIN TECHNIQUES FOR ANALYZING SURVEYS AND THEIR ADVANTAGES AND DISADVANTAGES

Four of the main techniques used to analyze surveys are frequencies, crosstabs, means, and graphs, which have the following advantages and disadvantages.

Frequencies

Frequencies involve counting the number of instances for each of the categories of each variable and finding the percentages for each category based on the number of people in the survey or the number answering a question. Frequencies can be used for individual or multiple variables and for both descriptive and evaluative research.

For example, in looking at gender, one might look at the percentage of the sample that are males and females; in looking at age, one might look at the percentage of people in each age group. Another example of using frequencies is determining the percentage of people choosing a particular action in a forced choice question.

The advantages of using frequencies is that this is a simple way to provide an overview of responses to a questionnaire. Also, the frequencies for the categories can be combined to create a cumulative percentage for variables when the categories can be grouped together, such as age groups or the amount someone has spent on something.

A disadvantage of using frequencies is that if there are multiple choices for different categories, the percentages will add to more than 100%, making it difficult to compare responses across samples. Another disadvantage is that responses to multiple questions will result in multiple frequency, percentage, and cumulative percentage charts, which can be unwieldy for presenting the data. Also, using frequencies doesn't work well when there are numerous categories for ordinal or Likert-type variables.

Crosstabs

Crosstabs involve conducting a cross-tabulation of two or more variables to look at the relationship between those variables, an approach commonly used in explanatory and evaluative research. For example, one might do a cross-tabulation between a demographic variable, like age or gender, to see if different groups differ in their response to a question, such as if an activity appeals more to younger or older age groups or to men or women.

The choice of which total to use in percentaging a row or column depends on the data, based on which comparison one makes, such as if one compares the demographic breakdown for a particular activity or compares the activity preferences for members of a demographic group.

Besides doing a two-way cross-tabulation, one can use a three way cross-tabulation or create even more cross-tabulations, if the sample size is large enough. For example, one can look at the sex and age breakdown for different activities.

The advantage of using crosstabs is that one can compare differences between different groups, and the results can be used in explaining these differences. Crosstabs can also be used to compare how different user and customer groups respond in evaluative research.

The disadvantage of crosstabs is that this method can lead to creating a very large number of tables when there are multiple responses, due to the many ways the variables can be cross-tabulated with each other. Also, not all the crosstabs may be meaningful, although it may not be clear which ones are meaningful until one has done the crosstabs. Another disadvantage is the number of items that can be cross-tabulated is limited if there is a small sample size.

Means

Using means involves finding the mean or average for certain types of variables in all types of research – descriptive, explanatory, and evaluative. However, means can only be obtained for scales or ordinal data. It is not meaningful to find means for numerical codes for nominal variables.

The advantage of using a mean is that it can provide a single statistic, which can be used in comparing different responses, rather than looking at a frequency table, which shows the percentage of responses for different categories in ranking or rating something.

Using a mean can be problematic, however, if it has resulted from averaging widely different responses, such as when a large percentage of respondents strongly agree or strongly disagree with something. This result indicates a bimodal distribution, but using the average of the two disparate results would make it appear that the respondents have a neutral response, rather than a widely divergent one, since these differences are averaged together.

A mean is also a disadvantage when there are a few extreme cases, such as when a few people with a very high income skew the whole distribution, so the average income is much higher for everyone. In such cases, a median might be a more accurate statistic, since it more accurately reflects the middle point of the data.

Graphs

Graphs are a way to present the results of an analysis in graphic form, such as a bar graph, stacked bar graph, pie chart, line graph, or scatterplot. The bar graph, also called a histogram, is one of the most common methods of presenting data in social research. It shows the number or percent of cases on one axis of the graph and the category being measured on the other.

If two variables are cross-tabulated with each other, these results can be shown on a stacked bar graph, in which one variable is shown in one color or pattern and the other variable is shown in another, so together they make up a total stack for each of the categories into which the variable is divided. An additional variable might be shown by two side by side stacks, such as for a study conducted in two cities or in two different years.

The advantage of using a graph is that it shows visually the count or percentage differences in the results for different variables, rather than just presenting the count or percentages in a table.

A disadvantage is that a graph can be misleading, depending on how it is drawn to show differences between groups. For example, if there is a great difference between groups, but the percentage categories on the side are shown close together, this might underplay the differences. Conversely, if there are only small differences, spacing the percentages far apart could make the differences seem greater than they are. It might also be hard to know the actual percentages unless they are written in or on top of the bars.

Pie Charts

Pie charts are a type of graph which divide up the number, percentages of categories, or responses for a variable into the sections of a pie. The advantage of a pie chart is that it shows the relative size of the different responses when there is a meaningful total, such as 100%. However, a pie chart doesn't work well when there are multiple responses, so the total is greater than 100%.

CHAPTER 13

THE MAJOR STATISTICAL CONCEPTS

If you are going to do research in the leisure and social science field, the major statistical concepts are these:

Probabilistic Statements

These are statements about a population which are drawn from the results of a sample; they can only be probable and not certain, because we can never know if a sample drawn from a population fully represents that population, since it is only a subset of that population. As a result, we can only estimate how probable it is that those statements really represent or are true of that population, using statistical measures to determine the probability.

The three types of probabilistic statements that can be made about a population based on a sample are descriptive, comparative, or relational statements.

- A descriptive statement is a general characterization of the results, such as stating that a certain percentage of a group engage in an activity.

- A comparative statement compares the results of one group to another, such as stating that a certain percentage of the members of one group participate in an activity while a different percentage of the members of another group participate in that activity.

- A relational statement refers to a relationship between being a member of one group and another group and having a certain characteristic or participating in a certain activity. For example, one might state that the members of one group are more likely to have a certain trait or participate in an activity compared to the members of another group.

Normal Distribution

A normal distribution is the bell shape curve that results from drawing a repeated number of samples and plotting the results of each sampling, so that the population's percentage or average is in the middle of the distribution, while the sample's percentage or average is plotted on the curve and compared to the population's percentage or average. Then, depending on the size of the sample, a statement can be made about the probability that the statistic for the sample reflects the statistic for the population.

Commonly the 5% or 95% level is used in social and leisure research to indicate that something is significant at this confidence level, meaning that we are 95% sure that this sample statistic does reflect the statistic for the population, and there is a 5% chance that this result doesn't reflect the population's statistic. However, sometimes a higher significance level is used, showing an even greater confidence in the results, such as using a 1% or 99% level, if a very large sample is drawn in a study.

Significance

This concept is the degree to which a difference or relationship observed in a research study is not likely to have occurred by chance. For example, the significance of a finding is assessed when two percentages or means from two groups are compared, such as if one compares males and females or members of different age groups on whether they participate in a certain activity. The greater the difference between these percentages or means, the more likely it is that these differences are significant and not just due to chance.

Null Hypothesis

This is the hypothesis in a study which states that a difference or relationship is not significant, whereby the alternate hypothesis or a series of alternate hypotheses state that a difference or relationship is significant at the level of significance chosen for the study. To show there is a significant difference, a study is designed to disprove the null hypothesis of no significance in order to accept the alternative hypothesis that the research finding is significant at that level. If there is only a small difference between percentages or means, this indicates that the null hypothesis of no difference is probably correct at the study's level of significance.

Independent and Dependent Variables

These are variables that are related to each other, in that the changes in the independent variable affect, influence, or cause changes in the dependent variable. For example, if income is positively related to participation in a sports activity, an increase in income will lead to greater participation in that activity; if income and participation are negatively related, an increase income will lead to less participation in that activity.

Correlation

This is a statistical approach of looking at the way in which two or more scale or ordinal variables relate to each other. If there is a systematic relationship between them, they are considered to be correlated. If they are positively correlated, the dependent variable will increase when the independent variable increases.

Conversely, if they are negatively correlated, the independent and dependent variables will increase or decrease in opposite directions. In other words, there is a negative correlation between the variables if the dependent variable increases when the independent variable decreases, or if the dependent variable decreases when the independent variable increases.

This relationship can be shown graphically on a scatterplot, in which a dot shows the relationship of two variables for each individual case or observation.

CHAPTER 14

THE MAJOR DATA ANALYSIS TECHNIQUES

The major data analysis techniques to use in social research are the following. Choose the appropriate one to use for your study.

Chi-Square Test

This test, signified by the symbol X^2, shows the relationship between two nominal variables, which describe something, such as one's gender or age. This test is designed to show if the relationship is significant or not by rejecting the null hypothesis of no difference at a certain level of confidence – commonly 95%. The Chi-Square test involves examining the counts or percentages in the cells of a table and comparing the actual counts with the expected counts, which would occur if there was no significant difference. For example, if one conducts a study with an equal number of people of two different ethnic groups about their participation in two activities, one would expect the same number of members in each group in each activity if there is no difference. However, if one activity is more popular with one group and the other activity is more popular with the other, the percentage interested in each activity would be significantly different.

In short, a Chi-Square test is done by summing up the differences between the actual counts or percentages and the expected counts or percentage to get the squared values of the differences. The larger the total, the bigger the Chi-square value, and the more likely there is a significant difference.

T-Test

This test involves comparing two means to determine if the differences between them are significant, based on rejecting the null hypothesis of no difference and accepting the alternative hypothesis that there is a difference. For example, a T-test might look at the average income of people participating in different activities, such as playing golf versus going bowling, to see if the income of the two groups differs, which might be expected, since golf is an expensive sport while bowling is a relatively inexpensive one.

The T-test can be conducted as a paired samples test or an independent samples test. In the paired samples test, the means of two variables for everyone in the sample are compared, such as the amount of time spent on the Internet versus the amount of time watching TV. By contrast, in the independent samples test, the means of two subgroups in the sample are compared in relation to a single variable, such as the amount of time teens and parents spend on the Internet, to see if there are any differences between them.

One-Way Analysis of Variance or an ANOVA Test

This test compares more than two means in a single test, such as comparing the means for males and females for a number of activities, such as how much time each group spends eating out, using the Internet, watching TV, going shopping or participating in sports. The test examines whether the mean for each variable in the test is different or the same compared to the overall mean, and therefore either significant (so the null hypothesis is rejected and the alternate hypothesis is accepted) or there is no difference (thereby affirming the null hypothesis).

The one-way test not only considers the differences between the means for the overall population and for the different subgroups, but it examines the differences between the means, which is called the "variance." This variance is determined by summing the differences between the individual means and the overall mean to get the results, which are interpreted in this way. The higher the variance <u>between</u> groups, the more likely there is a significant difference between the groups, whereas the higher the variance <u>within</u> groups, the less likely there is a significant difference between the groups. The F score represents the analysis of these two difference measures of variance to show the ratio between the between groups and the within groups variance.

In conducting this analysis, one needs to take into consideration the number of groups and the size of the samples, which determine the degrees of freedom for that particular test. The result of these calculations produces an F score. The lower the F score, the more likely there is a significant difference between the means of the groups.

Factorial Analysis of Variance

This is another ANOVA test, which is based on analyzing the means of more than a single variable, such as examining the relationship between participation in an activity and the participants' gender and age. The test involves cross-tabulating the means of different groups to determine if they are significant by comparing the means of the groups and the degree of spread between the groups. The degrees of freedom are taken into consideration along with the sum of the squares to produce a square of the means and then an F score. The lower the score, the greater the likelihood of a significant difference between the group means.

Correlation Coefficient (usually designated by "r")

This test shows the degree of correlation between two variables. The coefficient ranges from 0 when there is no correlation to +1 if the correlation between two variables is perfect and positive or -1 if the correlation is perfect and negative. The numbers between 0 and +1 or -1 indicate the degree of positive or negative correlation between the variables. The size of r is determined by calculating the mean for each variable and examining how far each point of data is on the x and y axis from the mean in a positive or negative direction. Then, one multiplies the two differences, and takes into consideration the size of the sample to determine how significant r is at a predetermined level of significance (usually the 95% or 5% level).

Linear Regression

This approach is used when there is a sufficiently consistent correlation between two variables, so that a researcher can predict one variable by knowing the other. To this end, a researcher creates a model of the relationship by developing an equation that describes this relationship. This equation is generally stated as $y = a + bx$, in which "a" is a constant, and "b" refers to the slope of the line that best indicates the fit or correlation between the two variables being measured.

Non-Linear Regression

This refers to the relationships between two variables which do not have a linear relationship, so that a single straight line can't express their relationship. Such a non-linear regression might occur if there is a curved relationship, such as when there is a gradual growth of interest in an activity, followed by a spurt of enthusiasm, and then a plateau of interest. Another example might be a bimodal distribution, such as when interest in an activity peaks twice a year or experiences an up and down growth of interest. Still another example of a non-linear regression is a cycle relationship, which might occur when a spike of interest follows the introduction of a new program several times a year, followed by a decline in interest until a new program is introduced again.

Factor Analysis

This method involves determining what variables might occur in combination with one another, such as if people who like to snorkel dive also like to surf and water ski, suggesting that an underlying factor for an interest in both activities might be an interest in water sports. A factor analysis can be done by using a correlation matrix to group the variables together and see which ones have the largest correlation with one another.

Cluster Analysis

This method involves grouping individuals together, such as by combining several income categories related to a particular variable (i.e., participating in an activity). Then, one seeks to create a smaller number of groups, such as having a low, medium, or high income, that show a similar pattern of relationship to that variable. The analysis is done by combining the data points which are closest together into a cluster and repeating the process to combine previously formed clusters until there are only a few or even just two clusters. The result of this process is a dendogram, which looks like a series of elimination rounds from quarter finalists to semifinalists to finalists in a competition, though in this case the repeated clustering selects the key meaningful divisions for a particular variable.

CHAPTER 15

THE EASIEST METHOD FOR SOCIAL RESEARCH

The easiest to use statistical method for social researchers, particularly if a quick analysis is needed to make a decision, is the Chi-Square test, since it looks at a cross-tabulation of frequencies to determine the relationship between two nominal variables. This method is most useful for general research findings. While accuracy is necessary, a high level of precision is not needed.

Another reason a Chi-square test would be especially useful is that questionnaires are often used to determine the number of people from different groups participating in different activities or their preferences for different services, products, or activities. For example, a recreation center manager might want to find out which activities are most popular among males and females to decide which activities to offer in an upcoming program, as well as how to best promote these activities to the most likely participants. To this end, the questionnaire might ask a sample of males and females which activities on a list they would prefer to participate in. A cross-tabulation would then show the count of the males and females selecting a particular activity, and the researcher could determine the percentage of males and females selecting each option. A Chi-square test would show if there were significant differences between the males and females in their preferences. If so, the recreation manager might target certain activities to males and others to females, or if there were no significant differences, the recreation manager might promote this as an activity for both.

However, while the Chi-square and other statistical tests might be used to determine the significance of any differences, commonly the managers of organizations in many fields, such as recreation and tourism, don't use statistical tests, even for a survey with scale and ordinal data, since much of the research in the field is descriptive.

The test has some weaknesses, however. It can only be used with two variables which are cross-tabulated with each other, so one can't look at the interaction between variables. For instance, if one wants to look at the relationship between age and gender on participating in a particular activity, one can't do so in a single test. One would have to look at the relationship between age and an activity in one table, and the relationship between gender and that activity in another. Likewise, if one wants to look at the relationship between participating in an activity, distance from the location, and gender, one can't use a single table. Instead, one would have to create different tables for each crosstab.

Another weakness is the Chi-square test can only be used with nominal data based on the count or percentage in different categories of a variable. It cannot be used with scale or ordinal data that has been combined to create a summary result, such as an average, mean, or a median, like the median income of individuals participating in different activities.

Another weakness of the Chi-square test is that it can be easier to make comparisons for multiple categories by using summary data, rather than breaking down the data by cell counts and percentages. For instance, to look at preferences for a number of different programs, it would be easier to look at a mean showing the preference for each program for each group in a single table, rather than having separate cross-tabs to show the preferences of males and females or of individuals with different backgrounds. It would then be easier to make a decision about how to offer the different activities, programs, or services based on this summary data rather than looking at numerous crosstabs with percentage or count breakdowns.

References

"The Impact of Participation in an Inclusive Adventure Education Trip on Group Dynamics" by Sue Sutherland and Sandra Stroot in the *Journal of Leisure Research*, 2010, Vol. 42, No. 1, pp. 153-176.

"'You don't want to hurt his feelings...': Family Leisure as a Context for Intergenerational Ambivalence," by Shannon Hebblewaite and Joan E. Norris in the *Journal of Leisure Research*, 2010, 42, No. 1, pp. 489-508.